MAY YOUR HEARTS BLOSSOM

An address by

SRI MATA AMRITANANDAMAYI DEVI

At the Parliament of the World's Religions,
Chicago, September 1993

May Your Hearts Blossom
An Address by Sri Mata Amritanandamayi
At the Parliament of the World's Religions,
Chicago, 3rd September 1993.

Translated by
Swami Amritaswarupananda

Published by
Mata Amritanandamayi Mission Trust
Amritapuri, Kollam Dt. 690 525
Kerala, India
Website: www.amritapuri.org
Email: info@theammashop.org

Copyright © 1994 by Mata Amritanandamayi
Mission Trust

All rights reserved. No part of this publication
may be stored in a retrieval system, transmitted,
reproduced, transcribed or translated into any
language, in any form, by any means without the
prior agreement and written permission of the
publisher.

First edition: March 1994, 2000 copies
Eighth edition: July 2007, 2500 copies
Ninth edition: May 2009, 2000 copies
Tenth edition: July 2014

Contents

A Portrait of the Divine Mother	4
The Second Parliament of the World's Religions – 1993	7
The Assembly of Presidents	11
Prelude	13
The Flow of the Ganges	17
May Your Hearts Blossom	20
The Glorious Legacy of Sanatana Dharma	44
The Message of Sanatana Dharma	50
Towards a Global Ethic	56

A Portrait of the Divine Mother

Here is a mystic accessible to anyone and everyone, with whom you can converse and in whose presence you can feel God. She is humble, but firm as the Earth. She is simple, yet beautiful like the full moon. She is the embodiment of Love, Truth, renunciation and self-sacrifice. She not only teaches, but practices Her teachings every moment of Her life. She is a giver of everything and the receiver of nothing. She is a Great Master and a Great Mother. Such is Mata Amritanandamayi Devi.

Mother was born in full awareness of the Supreme Truth. Having undergone or displayed (we know not which) the most rigorous spiritual discipline, She embraced the entire world with

A Portrait of the Divine Mother

love and compassion of indescribable dimensions, the love and compassion that is Her very essence and being.

From Her tender childhood, the love of God consumed Her. Without a Guru or guide, She immersed Herself in the quest for the Divine Mother and Father. She withstood constant mistreatment from Her family, villagers and skeptics, all of whom failed to comprehend Her innate greatness. Alone in the midst of this battlefield, She confronted everything unperturbed, with steadfast courage, patience and enduring love for all. At the age of 21, She outwardly manifested Her state of Oneness with the Supreme, and at 22, began to initiate seekers of Truth into spiritual life. By the age of 27, the Divine Mother had established the spiritual headquarters of Her international Mission, in the house where She was born. Five years later, there were nearly 20 branch ashrams throughout India and abroad. And in 1987, in response to an invitation by Her devotees in America and Europe, the Divine Mother made Her first world tour, inspiring and uplifting countless people around the globe. She was then 33 years old.

Amma's entire life is an incomparable example of selfless, unconditional love. Throughout decades of tireless service, Amma has personally counseled and consoled millions of suffering people from all walks of life and from every corner of the globe. Mother wipes their tears with Her own hands and removes the burden of their sorrows. The personal touch, the warmth, the compassion, tenderness and deep concern Amma shows constantly for everyone, the spiritual charisma, innocence and charm ever so natural to Her are all unmistakable and unique. To Mother, each and every being in this universe is Her own child. As Mother Herself has said:

"An unbroken stream of Love flows from Amma towards all beings in the universe. This is Amma's inborn nature."

The Second Parliament of the World's Religions – 1993

> *"Though different streams spring from different sources, all mingle their waters in the same sea. O Lord, the different paths which people follow, various though they may appear, they all lead to Thee."*
>
> —Atharva Veda

The spirit of all religions is one. They share the same fundamental values. They share a common concern for the universal welfare of all beings, and an acceptance of the innate sacredness of all life.

The Hindus look upon all beings as divine; Christians preach universal love; Shintoists revere the life and rights of everyone; Jains declare all life to be interrelated and mutually supportive; Sikhs hold that to serve everyone is to worship the Divine; the Koran affirms the equality and unity of all mankind; and Buddha says that the distinctive signs of every true religion are goodwill, love, purity and kindness.

Yet, throughout the ages, more battles have been fought and more blood has been spilled upon the earth in the name of religion than for any other cause.

The first Parliament of the World's Religions was held in Chicago in 1893. It marked the first concerted effort to bring all the different religions to a common platform where leaders and representatives of all faiths were able to communicate and share their views. At that first conference they explored the possibilities for religious tolerance and harmony, and ways in which they could cooperate in order to solve the burning issues that beset humanity.

The 1893 Parliament of the World's Religions was attended by 400 men and women, representing 41 religious traditions. It was there that Catholicism and Judaism were recognized as major American religions, and that Hinduism and Buddhism were first introduced to the West. And, it was on this occasion that Swami Vivekananda won wide recognition for India's ancient culture, philosophy and faith through his powerful words.

The centenary of the first Parliament of the World's Religions was held, also in Chicago, from August 28 to September 4, 1993. Over 6500 delegates, representing approximately 125 of the world's religions participated in the grand Parliament; among them were approximately 600 world spiritual leaders.

Unlike the first Parliament, more stress was laid on inter-religious dialogues than individual speeches as participants strove to embrace the consensus that exists among their religions. It was agreed that religion should be integrated with science, spirituality and other practical aspects of daily life, and that people of all faiths should be encouraged to share the fruits of their achievements with those who are less fortunate than themselves.

Whereas the first Parliament resulted in the acceptance of Jews and Catholics into the mainstream and a stirring introduction to the religions of the East, this second Parliament marked the growing recognition and influence of these other traditions and faiths. The Parliament provided a lucid example of an emerging religious pluralism.

During the eight-day Parliament, nearly 800 programs were held; among them were speeches, workshops, inter-religious debates, meditation lessons and cultural performances. Opportunities were also created for mutual participation in religious services and ceremonies.

The Parliament addressed many of the critical issues which now confront mankind. Environmental pollution and the nuclear threat, the widening gap between rich and poor, racism, oppression and the changing roles of men and women—these were some of the topics which were contemplated and discussed.

The overwhelming success of the Second Parliament of the World's Religions was in itself an affirmation of the message of harmony and co-operation that lies at the core of the world's religions.

The Parliament marked a great step towards the goal it initially envisioned: *"The purpose of the Parliament has never been to solely celebrate a watershed event in world history, but to add a fresh voice and dimension to the interfaith movement, to explore new avenues for lasting peace and to shape a vision for the new century."*

The Assembly of Presidents

A momentous achievement of this second Parliament was the formation of a core group of the world's most influential religious leaders, an assembly of 25 presidents representing all major faiths. During the days of the Parliament, this group met privately to discuss the problems facing the world, to propose solutions, and to set down a Global Ethic.

It was envisioned that this core group should work as a sort of spiritual United Nations: whenever a conflict arises anywhere in the world owing to religious intolerance, the group will use their collective influence and spiritual weight in order to find a peaceful solution. They will try to demonstrate to the world that religion can and should be a source of harmony rather than strife.

Divine Mother Amritanandamayi Devi was chosen as one of three presidents to represent the Hindu faith, the other two presidents being Swami Chidananda Saraswati (President of the Divine Life Society) and Sivaya Subramuniya Swami (Spiritual leader of the Saiva Siddhanta Church and publisher of Hinduism Today).

This distinguished assembly of presidents, who represent our many different paths, will strive not only to propagate interfaith dialogue, but also to lead humanity towards a new era of harmony and peace.

Prelude

On the 3rd of September, 1993, on the occasion of the centenary gathering of the Parliament of the World's Religions, Mother spoke on the great need for love and compassion in today's world.

Long before Mother's arrival at the Grand Ballroom of Chicago's Palmer House Hotel, hundreds of people had gathered in hushed excitement outside the great double doors. Mingling together was a collection of people from all parts of the world who had come to Chicago in order to attend the Parliament. Some were draped in the robes of various monastic orders, and others wore the ethnic dress of their countries; but most wore business suits or dresses and blended in with Chicago's mainstream. Among the crowd were press representatives for a variety of media, security guards who struggled to contain the continuous forward movement of the crowd, and of course, Mother's devotees, whose faces glowed in anticipation of Her arrival. Many commented that no other Parliament presentation had attracted nearly so many people.

The atmosphere was alive with hushed expectancy as this great ballroom full of people waited for the appearance of "one of the most revered spiritual teachers of modern India."

Mother arrived from the side of the stage wearing Her traditional white clothing and a striking garland of brightly colored flowers. In Her usual manner, She bowed to all those who had come, and sat down on the seat which had been specially arranged for Her. Who could have imagined that this unassuming woman, humbly bowing down before all the formalities of the Grand Ballroom of the Palmer House Hotel, was soon to express so wonderfully the latent yearning within everyone for the return of the soul.

Throughout the formal proceedings, there remained something childlike and innocent about Mother. Before beginning to speak, She told everyone that it was not Her way to deliver speeches, but that She would say a few words about things that She had experienced in Her own life. Then

Prelude

Her talk began—as bright and clear as the garland She wore, each point strung with brilliance to the next.

In Her speech, Mother emphasized the great need and urgency for religious principles to be assimilated into our lives. "The language of religion is the language of love. But it is a language the modern world has forgotten. This is the basic cause behind all the problems that exist in the present day world. Today we know only limited selfish love. Transformation of this limited love into Divine Love is the goal of religion. Within the fullness of true Love blossoms the beautiful, fragrant flower of compassion." This was the key note of Her speech. With Her characteristic simplicity and eloquence, Mother brought out the true spirit of religion and expounded its eternal principles in a way suitable for today's world.

Throughout Her speech, Mother emphasized the need for religion to become a balm for suffering mankind, rather than a breeding ground for egotism and rivalry. For one hour people sat enthralled, and when the speech came to an end, there was an outpouring of emotion which saw journalists in tears and complete strangers leaving their seats to come up to Mother.

In Her own inimitable way, Mother, having

dispensed with the formalities of talking, was now giving darshan.

People made their way forward, drawn like magnets towards Mother, yearning to share in this divine spirit which had so utterly touched them and inspired them. Mother greeted as many people as She could, tenderly embracing them one after the other, until sadly after just half an hour, they had to leave so that the formalities could proceed.

By Her mere presence, Mother had radiated the essence of the words and promises, ideas and intentions behind the Parliament of the World's Religions, making them come to life.

John Ratz, a Public Relations Counselor, while reflecting on the impact of the speeches delivered during the Parliament sessions, made this insightful observation *"Every other speaker had treated the subject of religion and spirituality as if they were two disparate entities. However, Amma's powerful words struck deep into the center of religion and spirituality, effacing the contradictions, bridging the gap and effecting a harmonious blend of both, thus unfolding their very essence. It was one of the most significant and powerful speeches."*

The Flow of the Ganges

Amma's speech was like the flow of the Ganges. From the highest peak of transcendent spiritual bliss, Amma spoke, letting others drink, bathe and swim in Her infinite consciousness, which overflowed through Her beautiful and compelling words.

As Amma, the very embodiment of Universal Love and Compassion spoke, a deep peace seemed to permeate the atmosphere. Her speech was intellectually convincing, and at the same time it had a tremendous healing power, a great purifying effect.

The Grand Ballroom of the Palmer House was packed with people from all walks of life who sat spellbound throughout Amma's speech. But when the address was over, hearts overflowed as people spontaneously rushed towards Amma to have Her darshan. It was a great and unforgettable occasion.

Swami Amritaswarupananda

MAY YOUR HEARTS BLOSSOM

An address by

**SRI MATA
AMRITANANDAMAYI DEVI**

At the Parliament of the World's Religions,
Chicago, September 1993

May Your Hearts Blossom

Salutations to all of you who have come here today, you who are the embodiments of Supreme Love. Words cannot express the gratitude that Amma feels towards the sincere organizers who have taken the time and energy to bring this highly beneficial conference into being. Though living in the midst of today's highly materialistic world, they have dedicated themselves to the organization of this conference which is based on the uplifting and sustaining values of religion. Through their hard work and prodigious efforts, they have set an example of selfless service by which the world can potentially profit. Before such big-heartedness Mother has nothing else to say, and humbly bows down.

It is not Amma's way to deliver speeches. Still, Amma will say a few words about things that She has experienced in Her own life. Amma asks your forgiveness, if there should happen to be any mistakes in what She says.

Religion is the faith which eventually culminates in the knowledge and experience that we ourselves are the all-powerful God. To lead man to the Realization of his own true state of Godhood, to transform man into God, that is the goal and purpose of Sanatana Dharma, India's "Eternal Religion", popularly known as Hinduism. At present, the mental lake is turbulent with the waves of thought. When these waves subside and die, that motionless substratum which shines forth is the essence of religion, the principle subject and goal of the philosophy of Advaita (non-duality). This motionless, unchanging principle is the very foundation of Sanatana Dharma. The great scriptural dictum, "Aham Brahmasmi" (I am Brahman, Absolute Consciousness), indicates the subjective experience of the non-dual Self.

"I am a Hindu", "I am a Christian", "I am a Muslim", "I am an engineer", "I am a doctor": this is how everyone speaks. That nameless, formless, all-pervasive principle common in all as the "I" is the Atman (the Self), the Brahman (the Absolute), or Ishwara (God). To deny the existence of God is to deny one's own existence. It is like saying with one's own tongue, "I have no tongue". God is present in each one of us, in all beings, in everything. God is like space. Space is everywhere. The entire creation exists in space. Suppose we build a house. Space exists before the house is built. And after its completion, the house exists in that same space. Even after the house is demolished, the same space remains. God too is like this. He exists, unchanging, in the past, present and future.

You may wonder, "If God is all-pervasive, then why am I not seeing Him?" Electricity cannot be seen, but put your finger in a live socket and you will experience it. In a like manner, God must be experienced to be known. Stand behind a tree and try to look at the sun. You don't see the sun, do you? You may say that the tree has covered the sun, but it is not so. The sun cannot be covered. Your eyesight is limited, that is why you do not see the sun. Similarly, even though God is everywhere, our limited vision prevents us from seeing Him. The attitude of "I" and "mine" has blocked our vision and bound our minds.

Sanatana Dharma does not ask us to believe in a God seated on a golden throne, high above the clouds. God is not a limited being. God is all-pervasive, omnipotent and omniscient. God is the Principle of Life and the Light of Consciousness within us. God, who is pure Bliss, is verily our own Self.

Mind alone is the cause of man's bondage and freedom. Religion is that principle which releases the mind from diverse thoughts and emotions, and from its dependence on external objects. It helps the mind to reach the state of eternal freedom or independence. It is the attitude of "I" and "mine" that makes us dependent. Practicing the principles of true religion is the path that will lead to the elimination of the ego.

We cannot expect to find happiness and perfection in the world. Yet people struggle all the time to find them in the world. Over the years, many women have been saying to Amma, "O Amma, I am forty and still I remain unmarried. I couldn't find a suitable man." The men also complain and say, "Amma, I have been looking for the bride of my dreams. But I haven't been able to find her." They lose hope and become dejected. It reminds Amma of a story.

Once, two friends met in a restaurant. One told the other that his marriage had been arranged, and he invited his friend to attend the wedding. He also inquired as to whether his friend had considered marriage. "Yes", replied the friend, "I was quite eager to get married and set out to find the perfect wife. I met a woman in Spain. She was beautiful, intelligent and spiritual, but she had no worldly knowledge, so I couldn't consider marrying her. In Korea I met another woman. She was beautiful, intelligent and had both worldly and spiritual knowledge, but I couldn't communicate with her. So again, I continued my search. Finally, I met her in Afghanistan—the woman of my dreams. She was perfect in all respects. I could even communicate with her." Interrupting, the first fellow inquired, "Did you marry her?" "No", replied his friend. "Why not?" asked the first fellow. "Because she, herself, was looking for the perfect husband."

What is it that human beings crave? They crave peace and happiness, don't they? People run here and there, seeking peace of mind. But peace and tranquillity have disappeared from the face of the earth. We are very enthusiastic in embracing the outside world and all its physical comforts. Meanwhile, the internal realm has become a living hell. There are more than enough comforts in the modern world. There is no scarcity of air-conditioned cars or air-conditioned rooms. These comforts are available everywhere on earth. But what a pity it is that the people who live in them still have no peace of mind. Many of them cannot sleep without the aid of pills. The restlessness and tensions of the mind have become so uncontrollable, so unbearable, that a number of people commit suicide even while living in the so-called lap of luxury, in these air-conditioned rooms. Those who show such a great interest in air-conditioning their cars and houses, should make some effort to air-condition their own minds. This is what is needed in order to attain real happiness.

Contentment and happiness depend solely on the mind, not on external objects or circumstances. Happiness really depends on self-control. Both heaven and hell are created by the mind. Even the highest heaven turns into hell if the mind is agitated; whereas, even the lowest hell will become a blissful abode for a man endowed with a peaceful and relaxed mind. Religion is the science which teaches us how to live a happy and blissful life while still living in this diverse world.

Faith and Alertness Are Needed in Today's World

These days, our faith is like an artificial limb. It has no vitality. We have no heartfelt connection with faith, for it has not been ingrained properly into our lives.

This is a scientific age. Intellect and reason have reached great heights. But surprisingly, the most intellectually developed people still have great faith and reliance only in cars, TVs, houses and computers—all of which could stop functioning and perish at any moment. We are deeply attached to these things and to the small comforts they offer. If they are damaged or destroyed, we hastily engage ourselves in repairing them. Yet we do not realize that it is actually we who are most urgently in need of repair. For we have lost faith in ourselves. We have lost faith in the heart and its tender feelings. A man who shows great patience in repairing his computer and TV, shows no patience in retuning the notes that are off-key in his own life.

Darkness is slowly enveloping the world. It is a pitiful scene we see all around. Having dissipated all their energy and vitality by running after objects of pleasure, people are collapsing. Man has gone beyond the reasonable limits set by nature. This does not mean that one should not enjoy the pleasures of the world. That is all right. But understand this great truth, that the enjoyment and happiness you get from sensual pleasures and worldly objects are only a minute reflection of the infinite bliss which comes from within your own Self. Know that your true nature is bliss. Just as today's newspaper will become tomorrow's waste paper, that which gives happiness today can easily become the source of tomorrow's despair. To understand this truth while living in the world is what religion teaches us.

The mind can be compared to a pendulum. Like the incessant movement of a clock's pendulum, the pendulum of the mind swings intermittently from happiness to sorrow and back again. When the pendulum of the clock moves to one extreme, it is only gaining enough momentum to swing back to the other end. Likewise, when the pendulum of the mind moves towards happiness, it is only gaining the momentum to reach the other pole of sorrow. Real peace and happiness can be experienced only when the pendulum of the mind stops swinging altogether. From that stillness ensues real peace and bliss. This state of perfect stillness is verily the essence of life.

Religion asks us to be constantly alert. A bird perched on a small twig is aware that at any moment, with the slightest breeze, the twig beneath it might break. So the bird is ever on the alert, ready to fly. Likewise, all of us are leaning on the objects of the world which can collapse at any moment. People ask, "Are you then telling us to abandon this world, to go to a secluded place and sit idle with our eyes closed?" No, that is not so. Be not lazy and lethargic. Perform your duties in the world. Engage yourselves in work. You can work to acquire wealth and to enjoy life, but try to remember that all this acquiring, possessing and preserving is like keeping a comb for a bald head. Irrespective of time and place, death will defeat us, snatching away all that we have. At the time of death, we will have to leave everything. Nothing or no one will come to our aid. Therefore, religion advises us: "Understand that the purpose of this precious life is not only to nourish your body, but to evolve to the state of Perfection."

If a person lives a life knowing and understanding the ephemeral nature of the world, he or she can still lovingly embrace life, without breaking down or losing all courage whenever difficulties arise. A person who does not know how to swim, is at the mercy of a turbulent ocean. Its waves can easily overpower him and pull him down into the depths. However, to play in the ocean is a delightful game for a person who knows how to swim. He cannot easily be tossed about by the waves.

In a similar manner, the diverse and contradictory nature of life is a delightful play for one who is aware of life's ever-changing nature. He can smilingly welcome both the negative and positive experiences of life with equal vision. But for those who do not have this awareness, life becomes an unbearable burden, filled with sorrow. True religious principles give us the strength and the courage to confront the difficult situations of life with a calm and balanced mind. Religion paves the way towards embracing this life with even greater joy, zest and confidence. For one who has truly imbibed the principles of religion, life is like the joyful play of an innocent child.

Today's world tries to evaluate religious principles by observing the actions of certain individuals, performed in the name of religion. They then judge the whole of religion based on the misdeeds of a few. This is like discarding the baby with the bath water. It is like condemning all medicines and doctors for the wrong prescription given by a single doctor. Individuals are sometimes good and sometimes bad. They have weaknesses and may lack discrimination. It is wrong to impose the faults and weaknesses that you see in them on the principles of religion.

It is the practice of religious principles that fills human life with vitality and energy. Without religion and faith, life on earth would be empty. Like a corpse adorned with an exquisite costume, the beauty and pleasures of life would be only superficial. Without religion, our minds become benumbed and barren. It is only because people have imbibed at least a little bit of religion and spirituality that there is still some beauty, vitality and harmony in our lives.

The Declining State of Religion Today

Religion contains the essential principles of life by which egotism and narrow-mindedness are eliminated. But sometimes, due to lack of proper understanding, the same religion becomes a breeding ground for these negative qualities. As a result of egotism, narrow-mindedness and competition, quarrels arise. They arise because people have failed to imbibe the essence of religion.

Today, there are thousands who are ready to die for their religion, but none who are willing to live by its principles. People do not realize that religion is something to be lived. They forget that it has to be applied and practiced in our day to day lives.

"My religion is the best! My religion is the greatest!" says one. "No, it is my religion that's the best and the greatest!" says another. Thus, the clamor continues. Because of this narrow vision and all the envy that exists, the true essence and message of religion is lost to the people.

Thinking of the present day quarrels which exist among religions, Amma is reminded of a story. Once, there were two patients staying in separate wards of the same hospital, and each one of them was being cared for by relatives. The patients were very ill and both were desperately crying out in pain. A relative of each went to obtain some urgently needed medication. Upon returning to the hospital, they met in a narrow doorway which could accommodate only one person at a time. Each person wanted to go through before the other, and neither of them would give way. Both insisted on being first, and a big quarrel ensued. While the patients were screaming in unbearable pain, their relatives continued to fight, each one still clutching the medicine in his hand. We often find the followers of different religions enacting the roles of these two relatives. Blinded by the external trappings of their faith, they fail to grasp its true essence and spirit. Instead of moving towards God, in the name of religion they actually drag themselves down.

This is the pitiful state of religion in the modern age. Owing to this unyielding and arrogantly competitive attitude, people have neither patience nor forbearance, and have lost their capacity to love.

All the members of a family will probably not be of the same nature or mental caliber. There may be one person who acts and speaks without discrimination or who gets extremely angry, thereby upsetting the entire household. But in the same family there may be one person whose nature is quiet and calm. He might be a person who is endowed with humility, sharp discrimination and great clarity of vision. Now the question is, who or what maintains the integrity and harmony of that family? Without much deliberation, one can easily reply that it is the latter's qualities of humility, discrimination and goodness that hold the family and its members together. One person's anger and lack of discrimination is balanced by another person's calmness, humility and prudence. Had the characteristics of the angry, indiscriminate family member prevailed, the family would have disintegrated long ago. Likewise, even though today's world is confronting a great threat, it is the patience, love, compassion, self-sacrifice and humility of the Mahatmas (Great Souls) which sustain and preserve the harmony and integrity of the world. The darkness of our age can be completely eliminated if, in each family, there is at least one member who is dedicated and willing to adhere to the essential principles of true religion.

When we truly imbibe the spirit of religion, the sorrow and suffering of others becomes our own. Compassion arises and we are able to sympathize with the pain and suffering of others. Only through the experience of oneness with the Self can we feel real compassion and concern.

Amma will tell a story. A person who lived in an apartment was suffering from cancer. Because of his affliction, he was crying and was in intense pain. He was so poor that he did not have enough money to buy a painkiller for a little relief from the agonizing pain. At the same time, in the adjacent apartment, another person was engaged in wanton enjoyment, seeking pleasure in alcohol, drugs, and through his association with women. If he had used the money he was wasting on destroying himself to help the poor man next door, the suffering of the sick man would have been mitigated. Furthermore, his own self-destructive tendencies and selfishness would have ended. To show compassion towards the poor and suffering people, that is our duty to God. Only such love, compassion and consideration would lead to harmony in the world.

If we accidentally happen to poke our eye with our own finger, do we punish the finger? No. We simply try to soothe the pain. Why do we not punish the finger? Because both are part of us, both are ours. We see ourselves in both the eye and the finger. In the same way, we should be able to see ourselves, our own Self, in all beings. If we can do this, we can easily forgive the mistakes of others. To be able to love and forgive others, seeing ourselves in them, seeing their faults as our own faults, that is the true spirit of religion.

Gold is in itself beautiful, lustrous and precious. But if it also had fragrance, how much more would be its value and charm! Meditation and religious or spiritual practices are indeed valuable. But if along with meditation and worship, one also has compassion for one's fellow men, it is like gold with a fragrance, something incredibly special and unique.

Religion is the secret of life. It teaches us to love, to serve, to forgive, to endure, and to interact with our brothers and sisters with empathy and compassion. Advaita (non-duality) is a purely subjective experience. But in daily life it may be expressed as love and compassion. This is the great lesson taught by the great saints and sages of India, the exponents of Sanatana Dharma.

The Role of Love and Compassion in Religion

True religion is a language forgotten by modern man. We have forgotten the love, compassion and mutual understanding taught by religion. The basic cause underlying all the problems that exist in the present day world, is the lack of love and compassion. All the chaos and confusion that prevail in an individual's life, at the national level and in the world as a whole, exist only because we have failed to practice true religious principles in our day to day lives. Religion should become part and parcel of life. Religion needs to be revived, it needs new life and vitality. Then only will love and compassion dawn within us. Love and compassion, alone, will wipe out the darkness, bringing light and purity to the world.

When love becomes Divine Love, the heart is filled with compassion. Love is an inner feeling and compassion is its expression. Compassion is expressing your heartfelt concern for someone, for a suffering human being.

There is love and Love. You love your family, but you do not love your neighbor. You love your son or daughter, but you do not love all children. You love your father and mother, but you do not love everyone the way you love your father and mother. You love your religion, but you do not love all religions. You may even dislike those of other faiths. Likewise, you have love for your country, but you do not love all countries, and may feel animosity towards different people. Hence, this is not true Love; it is only limited love. The transformation of this limited love into Divine Love is the goal of spirituality. In the fullness of Love blossoms the beautiful, fragrant flower of compassion.

When the obstructions of ego, fear and the feeling of otherness disappear, you cannot help but Love. You do not expect any return for your love. You don't care about receiving anything; you just flow. Whoever comes into the river of Love will be bathed in it, whether the person is healthy or diseased, a man or a woman, wealthy or poor. Anyone can take any number of dips in the river of Love. Whether someone bathes in it or not, the river of Love does not care. If somebody criticizes or abuses the river of Love, it takes no notice. It simply flows. When that Love overflows and is expressed through every word and deed, we call it compassion. That is the goal of religion. A person who is full of Love and compassion has realized the true principles of religion.

A compassionate person does not see the faults of others. He does not see the weaknesses of people. He makes no distinction between people who are good and people who are bad. When someone is full of Love and compassion, he cannot draw a line between two countries, two faiths or two religions. He has no ego. Thus, there is no fear, lust or passion. He simply forgives and forgets. Compassion is like a passage. Everything passes through it. Nothing can stay there, because where there is true Love and compassion there is no attachment. Compassion is Love expressed in all its fullness.

To see and feel life in everything, that is Love. When Love fills the heart, one can see life pulsating in and through the entire creation. "Life is Love"—this is the lesson taught by religion. Life is here. Life is there. Life is everywhere. There is nothing but life. So too, Love is everywhere. Wherever there is life, there is Love, and vice versa. Life and Love are not two, they are one. But ignorance about their oneness will prevail until Realization comes. Until Realization comes, the difference between intellect and heart will continue to exist. Intellect alone is not sufficient. In order to attain Perfection, in order to reach the fullness of life, one needs to have a heart filled with Love and compassion. To know this is the sole aim of religion and of religious practices.

This is the age of intellect and reason, the age of science. We have forgotten the feelings of the heart. A common expression the world over is, "I have fallen in love." Yes, we have fallen down into a love rooted in selfishness and materialism. We are unable to arise and awaken in love. If fall we must, let it be from the head to the heart. Rising up in Love, that is religion.

Restoring the Balance of Nature

True religion tells us that all of creation is a manifestation of God. If this is so, we must have love and concern for nature as well as for our fellow men. The scriptures say, "Isavasyamidam Sarvam": that everything is permeated with God-consciousness. The earth, trees, plants and animals are all manifestations of God. We should love them as we love our own Self. Actually, we should love them even more than ourselves, because only with nature's support can human beings exist. It is said that we should plant two trees for every one we cut down. However, when a large tree is replaced by two small seedlings, the balance of nature is not maintained. If a disinfectant is added to water in a smaller proportion than required, its effect will be minimized. If an ayurvedic medicine which is to be prepared with ten different ingredients is prepared with only eight, the medicine will not have the desired effect. Animals, plants, and trees all contribute to the harmony of nature. It is man's duty to protect and preserve them, for they are helpless to defend themselves. If we continue to destroy them, it will do the world great harm.

Mother remembers that in Her childhood cow dung would be placed directly upon the site of a vaccination in order to prevent infection. But today, cow dung will make a wound septic. Due to the toxins with which man has polluted the environment, our immune systems have become weakened, and the cow dung has also become harmful.

In times past, the life span of an ordinary person was over one hundred years, whereas nowadays, it is considerably less and still decreasing. There are rare cases today where people live for more than one hundred years, but this is usually accompanied by poor health and great suffering. Untreatable diseases have become prevalent due to man's transgression of the laws of nature.

How much pollution has been caused by the

smoke from factories? Mother is not suggesting that we close the factories; She is only saying that part of the profits should be used for devising methods to reduce pollution and to revive and protect the environment.

In olden days, rain and sunshine came at the right time and supported the cycle of growth and harvest. There was no need for irrigation because everything was taken care of by nature. Nowadays, we have strayed from the path of dharma (right action). We are not at all concerned about nature, and therefore, nature is reacting. The same cool breeze which once caressed mankind has now turned into a tornado.

We may doubt whether we have the power to restore the lost balance in nature. We may ask, "Are we human beings not too limited?" No, we are not! We have infinite power within us, but we are fast asleep and unaware of our strength. This power rises up when we awaken within. Religion is life's greatest secret which enables us to awaken this unlimited, but dormant inner power.

The Sanatana Dharma proclaims, "O man, you are not a tiny candle, you need not depend on someone else for your light. You are the self-luminous sun." As long as you think you are the body, you are like a small battery whose power is easily drained. But when you know yourself to be the 'Atman', you are like a giant battery connected to the cosmic power supply, which provides you with continuous and inexhaustible strength. When connected to God, the Self, the Source of all power, your energy never diminishes. You are able to tap into your infinite potential. Be aware of your own immense power and strength. You are not a meek little lamb, you are a majestic, powerful lion. You are the cosmic energy, the all-powerful God.

Children Should Be Taught Through Example

Amma has heard that many young children in the West carry guns when they go to school. She has been told that they may even shoot someone without any reason at all. Have you ever thought about why it is that young children are tempted to act in such cruel ways? It is because they have never been taught proper conduct. They have never been exposed to true love and compassion. Many boys and girls have come to Amma and said: "Our mother has not given us any love. Our parents have not taught us to behave properly. We have seen our mom and dad fighting with each other, right in front of us. As we witness such quarrels and selfishness, we begin to feel hatred towards the whole world. We become disobedient and selfish." Their parents, from whom they are supposed to learn the first lessons of love and patience, fail to set a proper example. It is Amma's request that parents should shower love and affection on their children in the early years. The infants should not be left uncared for in their cradles. Their mother's should hold them close and breast-feed them with love and tenderness. The children should be taught religious and moral principles during their formative years. Parents should not fight or express anger and hatred in front of their children. If they do, how is the child to learn patience and love?

If you walk through a field of soft, green grass, it will automatically make a path. Whereas, it would take countless trips up and down a stony hillside, in order to wear away a trail. In the same way, a child's character can easily be moulded. Children need loving care, but at the same time we should not forget to discipline them. Faith in God should be instilled in them, as well as love for the entire creation. This is possible only through proper religious education.

Children, our foremost duty and obligation in this world is to help our fellow human beings. God doesn't need anything from us. He is ever full. To think that God needs anything from us is like holding a lighted candle before the sun in order to light its way. God is the one who protects us;

He is not the one who needs to be protected by us. A river has no need for water from a stagnant pond. Rather it is the stagnant pond that needs the river's water, in order to become clean and pure. Today, our minds have become filled with impurities, like the stagnant pond. We need the Grace of God to purify and uplift us, so that we can selflessly love and serve the world.

To show compassion towards suffering humanity is our obligation to God. Our spiritual quest should begin with selfless service to the world. People will be disappointed if they sit in meditation, expecting a third eye to open after closing the other two. This is not going to happen. We cannot close our eyes to the world in the name of spirituality and expect to evolve. To behold unity while viewing the world through open eyes is Spiritual Realization.

When a flower has not yet blossomed, when it is still a bud, its beauty and fragrance are not yet manifest. No one is able to appreciate or enjoy them. But when the flower blossoms, when it unfolds in bewitching color and form, when its fragrance wafts through the air, it arouses joy and happiness all around. In the same way, the flowers of our hearts have not yet blossomed. They are still tiny buds. However, if nurtured by faith in God, by love and compassion, and by adherence to the principles of religion, the buds of our hearts are bound to unfold. Revealing their beauty and spreading their fragrance, they become blessings to the world.

Religion is not limited to the words of the scriptures. It is a way of life. Its beauty and charm are expressed in the love and compassion of those who live in accordance with its precepts. Whatever Amma has said until now, is like the script on the label of a medicine bottle. Simply reading the label will not effect a cure. The medicine has to be taken. You cannot taste the sweetness of honey by licking a piece of paper on which the word 'honey' has been written. Likewise, the principles described in the religious texts must be contemplated, meditated upon, and finally realized. Let us all take refuge at the feet of the Supreme Lord and pray that we may attain that state of Perfection.

The Glorious Legacy of Sanatana Dharma

> The following is a speech delivered by the Divine Mother before an audience of spiritual leaders and dignitaries, on the morning of the 4th of September, 1993, when the Hindu Host Committee honoured Her, by selecting Her as one of the three Presidents of the Hindu faith.

The great saints and sages of India who were the exponents of Sanatana Dharma have never claimed anything. Ever established in the supreme state of absolute fullness, they found it difficult to express the experience of the infinite Supreme Truth in words. They knew that the limitations of language would never enable a speaker to paint an adequate picture of the Truth. Therefore, the great ones always preferred to remain silent. Yet, out of compassion for those who are searching for God and those who are groping in darkness, they did speak. But before they spoke, they prayed thus:

> *"O Supreme Self, may my speech be rooted in my mind; may my mind be rooted in my speech."*

They prayed to the Supreme Brahman: "I am going to put my experience of the Truth into words. My experience of the Infinite Truth is so utterly complete that words cannot express it. But I am going to try. When I speak, give me the ability to express and convey the essential message of the Truth, through my words. Do not let me distort the Truth."

It is the duty of each one of us to transmit this great experience of the saints and sages to the world. It is very important that we respect the feelings and the faiths of people of other religions. But at the same time, we should also let the world know that the eternal Sanatana Dharma is not confined to certain individuals; it is a pure subjective experience of great importance to every human being. Everyone is the embodiment of this great Truth. Sanatana Dharma does not pertain to any particular caste, creed or sect. The world should know this. Truly, Sanatana Dharma is a great source of power and inspiration for all of mankind. As such, its followers should constantly work for the peace and harmony of the world. Only then will the sankalpa (resolve) of the Rishis become a reality.

The Rishis did not form a separate religion. They gave importance to different human values and spiritual truths. That is why their prayers, such as the following one, included the entire universe:

> *"Om Lokah samastah sukhino bhavantu."*
> May the whole world live in happiness.

> *"Om sarvesham svastir bhavatu*
> *Sarvesham shantir bhavatu*
> *Sarvesham purnam bhavatu*
> *Sarvesham mangalam bhavatu*
> *Om shanti shanti shanti"*
> May contentment prevail in all.
> May peace prevail in all.
> May perfection prevail in all.
> May auspiciousness prevail in all.
> Peace... Peace... Peace.

Once, a sannyasin was invited by a widower to pray for the peace of his wife's soul. The sannyasin began to pray: "Let everyone be happy; let there be no sorrow; let auspiciousness fill the entire universe; let everyone reach perfection, etc." The husband who was listening to the prayer became upset by this. He said to the sannyasin: "Swami, I thought you were going to pray for my wife's soul, but I haven't heard you utter her name even once." The swami replied: "I am sorry, but I cannot pray like that. My faith and my Guru have taught me to pray for everyone, for the entire universe. In truth, only by praying for the good of the whole world will the individual be benefited. If you water the branches of a tree, the water is wasted. It is only when the roots are watered that the nourishment reaches the branches and leaves of the tree. Only if I pray for everyone, will your wife receive her blessing. Only then will her soul find peace. I cannot pray in any other way." The swami was so convinced about this, that the husband had no choice but to yield to his wishes. The husband said, "All right, you can pray as you like. But can't you at least exclude my neighbor from your prayers." This is the prevalent attitude among the people of today. We have lost our ability and willingness to share.

When the cold war between Russia and America ended, there was a great sigh of relief throughout the world. With the commitment to end hostilities, the threat of a nuclear war, which could potentially destroy the world, was removed.

Now for the first time, families who were separated by the artificial boundaries of different political ideologies have been reunited in the spirit of love which had always bound them.

Of course, there are pockets of people involved in the manufacturing of weapons of destruction, people who are only concerned about their selfish ends.

The sole purpose of nature is to support creation. We should have faith and trust in this. We ought to search for alternative peaceful ways to earn our livelihood, rather than destroying one another for the sake of self-aggrandizement.

Merely going to temples, churches or mosques and performing worship does not constitute the whole of religion or devotion. We should be able to behold God, the Self, within ourselves and within all beings.

This is the dawn of the 21st Century. Here and now, let all the great sannyasins, spiritual leaders and the Hindu host committee, who worked so hard for the success of the religious Parliament, take the following oath, at least mentally:

"Regardless of time and place, we will work hard for the peace and harmony of the entire world, and to alleviate the suffering of humanity. In this way, let the great sankalpa of Sanatana Dharma become a living truth. And let us be determined to transmit this great Truth, and the essential principles of life, to all young men and women. They are the flower buds of the future generation, about to open and become the fragrance of the world."

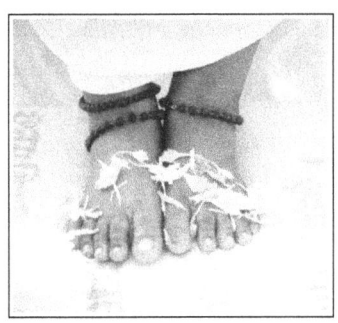

The Message of Sanatana Dharma

> The following message was sent by the Divine Mother for the Souvenir, "Reflections on Hinduism", which was published by the Hindu Host Committee, to commemorate the 1993 Parliament.

Religion gives what the world can never provide. What is it that man craves? What is it that is most absent in this world? It is peace, is it not? There is no peace anywhere, neither within nor without. To live life fully, one needs peace. And one needs love. Peace is not something which is gained when all desires are fulfilled. As long as the mind is there, desires will surface and problems will exist. Peace is something which arises when all thoughts subside, and you transcend the mind.

In that transcendental state, in which the individual self merges into infinite consciousness, the conceptual world of names and forms ceases to exist. This is the heart of the Hindu philosophy of Advaita (non-duality). Man can reach the ultimate state of Perfection. Indeed, this is his true nature. We may wonder why we do not realize this truth. It is mainly due to man's obsessive attachment to the external objects of the world. The ignorance about our real nature can only be dispelled by true knowledge. There is only one way for this pure knowledge to dawn, and that is through performing spiritual practices under the guidance of a Perfect Master, one who is eternally established in this transcendental state of bliss and peace.

A person who is filled with peace is relaxed. His life is balanced. He is never anxious or agitated. He does not grieve about his past. Because of his clarity of vision, he confronts every situation in life calmly and intelligently. His mind and his vision are not clouded by unnecessary thoughts. He will have problems in life, just as other people do, but the way a man at peace confronts them will be entirely different. His attitude will be different. There will be a special charm and beauty in all that he does. Even in the most difficult circumstances, he will remain unperturbed.

It is the nature of the human mind to vacillate. Like the pendulum of a clock, the mind is always moving from one thing to another. The movement is constant. The mind is always in a state of flux; at one moment it loves, the next moment it hates. The mind will like something in one moment, but in the next moment it will dislike the same thing. The pendulum of the mind sometimes moves towards anger, and then it moves towards desire. It cannot stop. It cannot be still. Because of the constant movement of the mind, the stable, unmoving, underlying ground of existence, which is the real nature of everything, cannot be seen. The movement of the mind creates incessant waves, and these waves, these ripples of thoughts, cloud everything.

Each thought, each emotional outburst, and each desire is like a pebble thrown into the mental lake. The incessant thoughts are like ripples on the surface of the water. The undulating surface makes it impossible for you to see through the water clearly. You never allow the mind to be still. Either there is the craving to fulfill a desire, or there is anger, jealousy, love or hatred. And if nothing is happening in the present, memories of the past come creeping in. Sweet pleasures, bitter memories, joyful moments, regret, revenge something will always arise. As soon as the past withdraws, the future comes with beautiful promises and dreams. Thus the mind is constantly engaged. It is always occupied and never vacant.

What you see is only the surface. You perceive only the waves on the surface. Yet, because of the movement on the surface, you mistakenly think that the bottom is moving too. But the bottom is still. It cannot move. You are superimposing the movement of the surface—the ripples of thoughts and emotions—onto the still bottom, the underlying ground. The movement caused by thought waves belongs only to the surface; it belongs to the mind. But to see this immovable substratum, the surface needs to become still and silent. The ripples have to stop. The vacillating pendulum of the mind must become still. To attain this still and peaceful state is the ultimate purpose of religion.

Once this stillness is attained, you can see clearly through the surface. You stop seeing disfigured forms. You behold the real ground of existence—Truth. All your doubts end. At this point you realize that you have been seeing only shadows and clouds. The purpose of religion is to help you behold the real nature of everything, while constantly abiding in the very depths of your own true Self. In that state all differences disappear and you see your own Self shining in and through every object.

Love for all humanity arises in one who has experienced the Truth. In that fullness of Divine Love blossoms the beautiful, fragrant flower of compassion. Compassion does not see the faults of others. It does not see the weaknesses of people. It makes no distinction between good and bad people. Compassion cannot draw a line between two countries, two faiths or two religions. Compassion has no ego. Thus there is no fear, lust or passion. Compassion simply forgives and forgets. Compassion is like a passage; everything passes through it, nothing can stay there. Compassion is love expressed in all its fullness.

God is Love, the life-force behind the entire creation. It is indeed rare to find a religion which does not consider love for all beings as the supreme factor. If religions adhered to this principle of Love, the differences seen today would become insignificant. God expects love, fraternity and co-operation from His children. Clinging to their superficial differences, human beings are paving the way for their own destruction.

Religion is supposed to spread the light of Love and Truth to humanity. Religion should not encourage separateness. There is only one Supreme Truth shining through all religions. Viewing religion with this attitude brings us closer to the

Supreme Truth, it helps us to understand each other, and it leads humanity towards peace.

How long are we going to live in this world? No one is going to live forever. Everything that we claim as our own is impermanent. If this is so, is it wise to waste this God-given life in pursuit of short-lived goals? The great masters of all religions unequivocally proclaim that there is a changeless substratum underlying this ever-changing world. It is through the realization of the Truth that immortality is attained. This is the ultimate purpose of life.

Religions should help people cultivate a strong desire to seek eternal life with a firm foundation of love and peace. This indeed is the greatest service which religion can offer humanity. Mutual love and co-operation between religions should be of primary importance in the world. Let love, peace, co-operation and non-violence be the beacons that light the way into the Twenty-first Century.

This is the essential message which the great lineage of saints and sages of India, and the eternal religion of Hinduism (Sanatana Dharma), gives to the entire world.

Towards a Global Ethic

> The following is the initial statement of the Declaration of a Global Ethic, a call for universal values, justice and compassion, signed by the majority of spiritual leaders who participated in the Parliament.

The world is in agony. The agony is so pervasive and urgent that we are compelled to name its manifestation so that the depth of this pain may be made clear. Peace eludes us, the planet is being destroyed, neighbors live in fear, women and men are estranged from each other, children die!

This is abhorrent! We condemn the abuses of the Earth's ecosystems. We condemn the poverty that stifles life's potential; the hunger that weakens the human body; the economic disparities that threaten so many families with ruin. We condemn the social disarray of the nations; the disregard for justice which pushes citizens to the margin; the anarchy overtaking our communities; and the insane death of children from violence. In particular we condemn aggression and hatred in the name of religion.

But this agony need not be. It need not be because the basis for an ethic already exists. This ethic offers the possibility of a better individual and global order, and leads individuals away from despair and societies away from chaos. We are women and men who have embraced the precepts and practices of the world's religions. We affirm that a common set of core values is found in the teachings of the religions, and that these form the basis of a global ethic. We affirm that this truth is already known, but yet to be lived in heart and action. We affirm that there is an irrevocable, unconditional norm for all areas of life, for families and communities, for races, nations, and religions. There already exist ancient guidelines for human behaviour which are found in the teachings of the religions of the world and which are the conditions for a sustainable world order.

We are interdependent. Each of us depends on the well-being of the whole, and so we have respect for the community of living beings, for people, animals, and plants, and for the preservation of Earth, the air, water and soil. We take individual responsibility for all we do. All our decisions, actions, and failures to act have consequences. We must treat others as we wish others to treat us. We make a commitment to respect life and dignity, individuality and diversity, so that every person is treated humanely, without exception. We must have patience and acceptance. We must be able to forgive, learning from the past but never allowing ourselves to be enslaved by the memories of hate. Opening our hearts to one another, we must sink our narrow differences for the cause of the world community, practicing a culture of solidarity and relatedness.

We consider humankind our family. We must strive to be kind and generous. We must not live for ourselves alone, but should also serve others, never forgetting the children, the aged, the poor, the suffering, the disabled, the refugees, and the lonely. No person should ever be considered or treated as a second-class citizen, or be exploited in any way whatsoever. There should be equal partnership between men and women. We must not commit any kind of sexual immorality. We must put behind us all forms of domination or abuse.

We commit ourselves to a culture of non-violence, respect, justice and peace. We shall not oppress, injure, torture, or kill other human beings, forsaking violence as a means of settling differences.

We must strive for a just social and economic order, in which everyone has an equal chance to reach full potential as a human being. We must speak and act truthfully and with compassion, dealing fairly with all, and avoiding prejudice and hatred. We must not steal. We must move beyond the dominance of greed for power, prestige, money and consumption to make a just and peaceful world.

Earth cannot be changed for the better unless the consciousness of individuals is changed first. We pledge to increase our awareness by disciplining our minds, by meditation, by prayer, or by positive thinking. Without risk and readiness to sacrifice there can be no fundamental change in our situation. Therefore we commit ourselves to this global ethic, to understanding one another, and to socially beneficial, peace-fostering, and nature-friendly ways of life. We invite all people, whether religious or not, to do the same.

We women and men of various religions and regions of the Earth therefore address all people, religious and non-religious. We wish to express the following convictions which we hold in common:

- We all have responsibility for a better global order.

- Our involvement for the sake of human rights, freedom, justice, peace, and the preservation of Earth is absolutely necessary.
- Our different religious and cultural traditions must not prevent our common involvement in opposing all forms of inhumanity and working for greater humanness.
- The principles expressed in this Global Ethic can be affirmed by all persons with ethical convictions, whether religiously grounded or not.
- As religious and spiritual persons we base our lives on an Ultimate Reality, and draw spiritual power and hope therefrom, in trust, in prayer or meditation, in word or silence. We have a special responsibility for the welfare of all humanity and care for the planet Earth. We do not consider ourselves better than other women and men, but we trust that the ancient wisdom of our religions can point the way for the future. We invite all men and women, whether religious or not, to do the same.

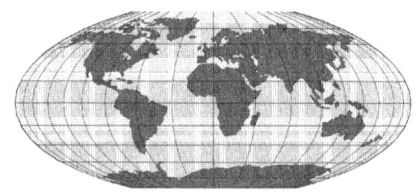

Book Catalog
By Author

Sri Mata Amritanandamayi Devi
108 Quotes On Faith
108 Quotes On Love
Compassion, The Only Way To Peace:
  Paris Speech
Cultivating Strength And Vitality
Living In Harmony
May Peace And Happiness Prevail:
  Barcelona Speech
May Your Hearts Blossom:
  Chicago Speech
Practice Spiritual Values And Save The
  World: Delhi Speech
The Awakening Of Universal
  Motherhood: Geneva Speech
The Eternal Truth
The Infinite Potential Of Women:
  Jaipur Speech
Understanding And Collaboration
  Between Religions
Unity Is Peace: Interfaith Speech

Swami Amritaswarupananda Puri
Ammachi: A Biography
Awaken Children, Volumes 1-9
From Amma's Heart
Mother Of Sweet Bliss
The Color Of Rainbow

Swami Jnanamritananda Puri
Eternal Wisdom, Volumes 1-2

Swami Paramatmananda Puri
On The Road To Freedom Volumes 1-2
Talks, Volumes 1-6

Swami Purnamritananda Puri
Unforgettable Memories

Swami Ramakrishnananda Puri
Eye Of Wisdom
Racing Along The Razor's Edge
Secret Of Inner Peace
The Blessed Life
The Timeless Path
Ultimate Success

Swamini Krishnamrita Prana
Love Is The Answer
Sacred Journey
The Fragrance Of Pure Love
Torrential Love

M.A. Center Publications
1,000 Names Commentary
Archana Book (Large)
Archana Book (Small)
Being With Amma
Bhagavad Gita
Bhajanamritam, Volumes 1-6
Embracing The World
For My Children
Immortal Light
Lead Us To Purity
Lead Us To The Light
Man And Nature
My First Darshan
Puja: The Process Of Ritualistic
  Worship
Sri Lalitha Trishati Stotram

Amma's Websites

AMRITAPURI—Amma's Home Page
Teachings, Activities, Ashram Life, eServices, Yatra, Blogs and News
http://www.amritapuri.org

AMMA (Mata Amritanandamayi)
About Amma, Meeting Amma, Global Charities, Groups and Activities and Teachings
http://www.amma.org

EMBRACING THE WORLD®
Basic Needs, Emergencies, Environment, Research and News
http://www.embracingtheworld.org

AMRITA UNIVERSITY
About, Admissions, Campuses, Academics, Research, Global and News
http://www.amrita.edu

THE AMMA SHOP—Embracing the World® Books & Gifts Shop
Blog, Books, Complete Body, Home & Gifts, Jewelry, Music and Worship
http://www.theammashop.org

IAM—Integrated Amrita Meditation Technique®
Meditation Taught Free of Charge to the Public, Students, Prisoners and Military
http://www.amma.org/groups/north-america/projects/iam-meditation-classes

AMRITA PUJA
Types and Benefits of Pujas, Brahmasthanam Temple, Astrology Readings, Ordering Pujas
http://www.amritapuja.org

GREENFRIENDS
Growing Plants, Building Sustainable Environments, Education and Community Building
http://www.amma.org/groups/north-america/projects/green-friends

FACEBOOK
This is the Official Facebook Page to Connect with Amma
https://www.facebook.com/MataAmritanandamayi

DONATION PAGE
Please Help Support Amma's Charities Here:
http://www.amma.org/donations

www.ingramcontent.com/pod-product-compliance
Lightning Source LLC
Chambersburg PA
CBHW061343040426
42444CB00011B/3067